ABSTRAKTION UND EINFÜHLUNG

Percival Everett

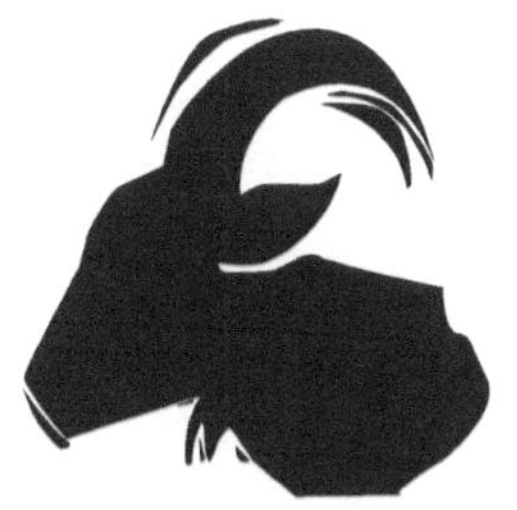

BLACK GOAT
LOS ANGELES

BLACK GOAT is an independent poetry imprint of Akashic Books created and curated by award-winning Nigerian author Chris Abani. Black Goat is committed to publishing well-crafted poetry and will focus on experimental and thematically challenging work. The series aims to create a proportional representation of female and non-American poets, with an emphasis on Africans. Series titles include:

Auto Mechanic's Daughter by Karen Harryman
Conduit by Khadijah Queen
Controlled Decay by Gabriela Jauregui
eel on reef by Uche Nduka
Gomer's Song by Kwame Dawes

For my sister, Denise, one of the best people I know

Published by Akashic Books
©2008 Percival Everett

ISBN-13: 978-1-933354-70-5
Library of Congress Control Number: 2008925946

Black Goat
c/o Akashic Books
Brooklyn, New York
Instagram, X, Facebook: AkashicBooks
info@akashicbooks.com
www.akashicbooks.com

The author would like to acknowledge the friendship and support of the series editor, Chris Abani. He is a young man who still has yet to tell the difference between bravery and foolhardiness. Thank you, Chris.

CONTENTS

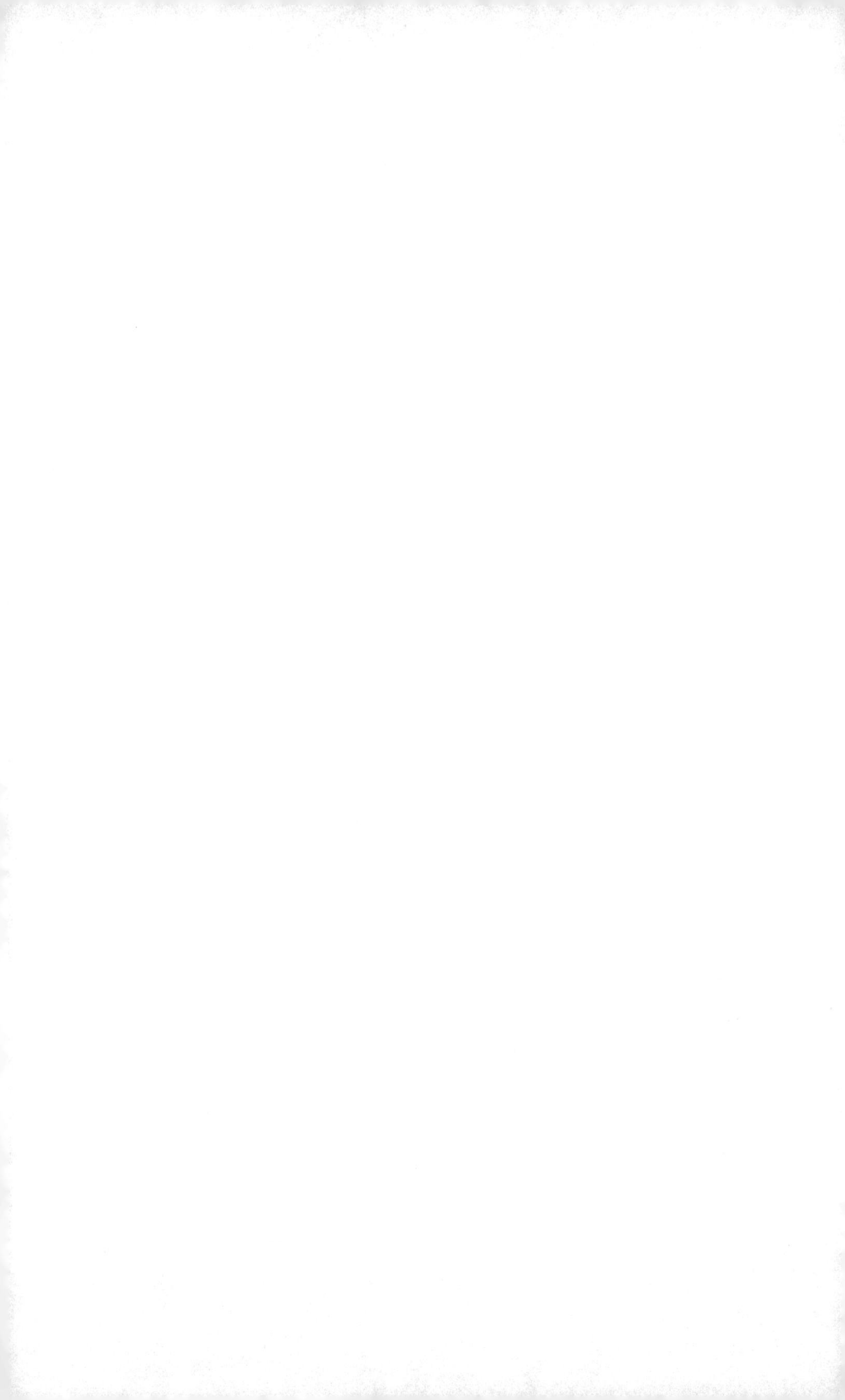

PICASSO 1916

1

Fingers are birds,
        Harlequin.

The costume Cocteau
        wore to visit.

But he was not persuaded
        to set his birds to
            flight,

unwilling to let another
        wear his guise.

Then with guitar, mask,
        sketchbook, 59 parades.

Parade all the becoming
        becomes the performing

and all the performing clowns
        on a public stage.

Laboratory left behind,
        Diaghilev breaks the glass

And the circus joins

     the high and low.

2

And all the performing becomes becoming,
all wishful thoughts and movements, the
performance being and being staying
put and waiting for context, substance.
Every performer knows, every one fears
that every meaning evolves a form,
that every form evolves an apology.

3

hairvery
maynining
ewolves
a forum

TABLEAU

1

Will the picture
exist in this frame?
Will I renounce not only
the focused gaze,
but the desire of my viewer?
The gaze is that old illusion.
The picture is nothing
but surface, nail, wire
and fictive shadow.

2

Unfocused gaze.
Untargeted sight.
Unaimed vision.
Lazy perception.
Errant sense data.
All on the floor, bathed
In available light.

3

hall
owned
the flour
baythieved

THE TRUTH

1

This
        is the first one.
There
        is no other.
Yet this,
        the first one,
this singular
        and only one,
is a fake.
        As I am a fake.
        As you are a fake.
        As I am a fake.

This singular

        and only

   one.

A equals A.

   X equals X.

   f(A) equals f(A).

How can a thing equal

           itself?

3

howl
kin
a thin
equell
hitself?

THE BLANK WALL

1

This art cannot exist of borrowed life.

And so that grand old lady and her smile take a beating.

Duchamp mustaches her,

Warhol replicates replicates her,

Léger gives her the keys.

Keys to get out of the frame, off the wall, or

keys to get in, back into the fray,

back into the gaze, into the gaze, into the gaze.

2

Léger gives her the keys.
        Sour-tasting metal behind closed lips.
Is she teething?
        We were all told she knew something.
The keys swallowed, they do no good,
        only keep entry away from others.
She touched her hair, flat palm,
        before or after, smiles still.

3

21

wee
wear
awl
towed
shay
gnu
stumpsting

BORROWED MASK

1

The only rule,
the only law
of genius, of imagination, of abandonment, of truth,
is change.

Not reworking, but change.

What is this borrowed mask?
The same old song once more?
Will Apollinaire defend us

                        this time?

As he did Renoir,
      his Arcadia, his nudes.
Who will bring back
the soul of art?
Who will bring it back
from the Underworld?
      Picasso having played
      Orpheus this go round.

2

Never rework,
the influence being imaginary
at best, but isn't that
enough?

Always new again,
though there is no new
                matter.
No new paint.
Only rearrangement.
No change.
Nothing to be changed.
No looking back.
No back upon which
                to look.

3

throw
thehair
kiss
know
knew
madher

A SPANISH MYTH

1

From the very moment of its

                     unveiling
it became what it would be to the century,
its story forced upon it, myth-lashed and tied,
at the Spanish pavilion, the Exposition in Paris,
screaming its rant from the horse's mouth,
screaming in the name of the suffering and
dead,
so also in the name of all humanity,
        perhaps even us.
Painting once again political, left to be gelded,
art discoursing its way back to irrelevance by
        word churning
over the possibility, the meaning of the possibility
          of stance
rather than the stance itself.

screaming its rant
            from the horse's mouth,
echoing through the canyon
      that is its own
            history.
Remember the loud crashes,
      booms,
recall the sickening cries,
   count them again with
      broad strokes
and nuanced gestures
and
   count your dollars
   and be safe.

3

27

wrycall
the stickineye
careyes

STUDIES

1

The creation of the work is ritual.
Mark the progress, document the stages,
photograph the metamorphoses and
recall, reglance these when interpretations
dig and cling too near and much to
the work in its final form.
Studies and notes at best loosely
connect, existing apart, world of their own.
If only the studies could scratch and claw
their way into the picture like vermin,
like ants, like cockroaches.
All this to find some privileged space,
and still what is the actual subject?

2

Dig and cling too near
to my own heart,

the work meaning nothing
upon departure,

the work meaning everything
upon departure.

If only these notes could
drag nails against pages' backs,

relieve some itch,
create some deep furrows

into which blood might
find its way with gravity.

3

derag
nayails
aginsty
payages
bax

BATHERS

1

We will
mimic the posture
of the living.

Or else allude
to the poses of some past,
progressively fading

as singular bodies
become part of the over
arching rhythm

of all things, rocks
and turtles, legs, hands,
almost, nearly,

not quite reproducing
the structural scheme
of nature itself.

Never lost in beauty,
but stranded on some bridge
between

where we were

and the viewer's constant

eye.

2

of all things,
rocks and turtles
hide along
the edge of this river.

one posing
as the other.
the turtle tries
to not be picked up.
the rock tries
not to be picked up.

3

hyde
aling
the hedge
dove
thist
ryeveer

GATE OF HELL

1

Stand before the door
of a museum not yet built.
Will this portal transcend
iconography?
Or be an exercise for fingers?

Open the door and there
are the people. Where
paintings go to die. Where
ideas are measured, weighed, lost
in a shuffle of slants.

2

There are the people
like ice cream in a cone,
filling it up all the way to the bottom,

standing on shoulders and heads.
The walls are pure space
and pure space is a joke,

a fucked fantasy,
a dirty eraser
that smudges when used.

3

a fugued
fantassee
a deartea
erazher

FOLIES BERGÈRE

1

There is no room for psychology.
                Not in this painted circus.
The barmaid has presence,
behind which which she withdraws
        as a person.

Baudelaire says of a soubrette,
                she has no thoughts,
receiving her view from
from the audience,

existing as she does
                for the pleasure
of others. Manet loves her.
But she will only mix
        drinks.

2

How unfair of Baudelaire
to say she has no thoughts.
Neither saucy nor coquettish,
she offers only what is sought.

Neither intriguing *in that way*
nor flirtatious, pert nor coy.
There is nothing frivolous in her act,
she's all work and no one's toy.

3

snore
fleertatious
peart
near
coi

GAUGIN PAINTS VAN GOGH

1

A
single
sunflower.

Not
in
the sun,

not
in
the ground.

Nature inside,
nature as art, decorations
of a kind,

being painted
by a painter
painting

a painter
painting a
sunflower.

"That's me," he
said, "I've gone
mad."

2

Being painted
by a painter painting
the painter painting
what is painted
in the act.

Paint, only paint,
wet paint, only wet
for a time, only time
will test the paint

that the painter
paints the painter
painting only
paint.

3

honely
thyme
well
teast
the painedt

KEEPS WATCH

1

The cloaked figure,
spine to a vertical line, right.

The woman, large, full,
savage? Diagonals the white bed.

The mottled wall behind
might be birds. Monster might be

beneath the bed. Her hands
flatten the pillow, her hair trails.

Death might be,
could be, lined up against a pillar.

2

Beneath the bed
        he stores canvases.
The soul of a thick-boned
        brown woman
scratched and stained
        and marking his travel
across her part of the ocean.

He waits for some door
        to open, for Renoir's ghost
to vacate this hall of the dead,
        for a friend to turn his head to hear.

3

scaratched
tan steined
und marocking
hi steravel

PURE FORM?

1

Let the paint
be music,
the analogy self-evident,
rubato, adagio con
espressione, the *scherzo,*
different keys, tempos,
signatures.
Let us dream
a music of colors,
pure form.
Pure form?
Untroubled,
unhampered
by contemplation of content.
Is it possible?
One language may
substitute for another
but nothing may
pass for,
displace,
supplant,
or answer for
a language.
Other languages
are all we have.

2

One language may
substitute for another,
but one is not as good as

                the next.
Some things can't be said.
Not an inadequacy of language,
      but a failure of speaking.
Not a bankruptcy of words,
      but a rupture in thought,
      a miscarriage of intent,
      a lead balloon.

3

knot
a banruptury
hove
weirds

THERE EXIST SOME X

1

The killer is in the house.
Six words.
Two nouns.
Two definite articles.
One verb.
One preposition.
Infinite meanings.
There is some house
and in it
there is a killer, but
not just any, but
the killer in *the*
house, yes, that
house and that
killer, who
perhaps is no
killer at all, but
a handsome woman,
a beautiful man,
a choice turn of phrase,
a dream and
the *house* is
my head, my world,
and of course
is is ironic.

2

That house
and that killer
on that block
of that street
in that city
in that culture
where irony is not salvation, but only salve.

3

wear
highrony
kiss
nut
slavation

PROCESS

1

The ritual of making
dies upon completion.

The body remembers,
like making love.

The body remembers
the gestures,

the midair changes,
the fall of an arm,

the angle of approach,
of withdrawal.

A calligraphy
survives completion,

but the making
is long long done.

2

The midair
changes
are the
tough
ones.

Catch me
before
I release,
if you please,
can.

3   56

eye
raylease

SHORT CIRCUIT

1

Eradicate the boundaries, obscure the edges,
collage, montage, assemblage, flying
in the face of the housing structure,
seeking at once inclusion and acknowledged exit.

The building has no permanence, the concept
of the building has no permanence, only
the event of the art, the ephemeral moment,
only itself, stealing from itself, from himself

and three others, the final illusion being
that any of it at all is ready-made.
That fuzzy, blurry, unfocused gaze on a
world personal yet never personalized.

2

The building
has no permanence.
What else is there
to say?

watt
hells
is theair
too
slay

RITUAL DANCE

1

One, thirty-one.
In the painting
                drip
        inside the painting
on every side
                edge
corner
        of the painting,
pointing the way
                        beyond the easel.

Pursue the rebirth
        of the archaic,
        painting in crisis,
                having hit the berg,
green ice floating,
        evoked as a rescue
                in the widening
                        wake of
an open-mouthed horse
and a bull on the left.

2

Beyond the easel
there is a forest of
aspens and firs
and trails that
go nowhere and
everywhere and
anywhere.

There are matted
hair bears,
musky moose,
and jays that have
no fear, only
feathers.

There is a canyon,
a river with trout
no one has seen
and will never see
and so they do not
exist.

There is darkness
that makes new stars
out of nothing

and weather that
is welcome and
more darkness.

3

wit
tearout
know
won
haze
sin